THE
PASSIONATE
LIFE

BIBLE STUDY SERIES

Matthew

OUR
LOVING
KING

12-WEEK STUDY GUIDE

BroadStreet
P U B L I S H I N G

BroadStreet Publishing Group, LLC
Racine, Wisconsin, USA
BroadStreetPublishing.com

The Passionate Life Bible Study Series
MATTHEW: OUR LOVING KING

© 2016 BroadStreet Publishing Group

Edited by Jeremy Bouma

ISBN-13: 978-1-4245-4920-7 (softcover)
ISBN-13: 978-1-4245-5253-5 (e-book)

Cover design by Chris Garborg at www.garborgdesign.com
Typesetting by Katherine Lloyd at www.theDESKonline.com

Printed in the United States of America

16 17 18 19 20 5 4 3 2 1

Contents

Using This Passionate Life Bible Study

The psalmist declares, "Truth's shining light guides me in my choices and decisions; the revelation of your Word makes my pathway clear" (Psalm 119:105).

This verse forms the foundation of the Passionate Life Bible Study series. Not only do we want to kindle within you a deep, burning passion for God and his Word, but we also want to let the Word's light blaze a bright path before you to help you make truth-filled choices and decisions, while encountering the heart of God along the way.

God longs to have his Word expressed in a way that would unlock the passion of his heart. Inspired by The Passion Translation but usable with any Bible translation, this is a heart-level Bible study, from the passion of God's heart to the passion of your heart. Our goal is to trigger inside you an overwhelming response to the truth of the Bible.

DISCOVER. EXPLORE. EXPERIENCE. SHARE.

Each of the following lessons is divided into four sections: *Discover the Heart of God*; *Explore the Heart of God*; *Experience the Heart of God*; and *Share the Heart of God*. They are meant to guide your study of the truth of God's Word, while drawing you closer and deeper into his passionate heart for you and your world.

The *Discover* section is designed to help you make observations about the reading. Every lesson opens with the same three questions: What did you notice, perhaps for the first time? What questions do you have? And, what did you learn about the heart of God? There are no right answers here! They are meant to jump-start your journey into God's truth by bringing to the surface your initial impressions about the passage. The other questions help draw your attention to specific points the author wrote and discover the truths God is conveying.

Explore takes you deeper into God's Word by inviting you to think more critically and explain what the passage is saying. Often there is some extra information to highlight and clarify certain aspects of the passage, while inviting you to make connections. Don't worry if the answers aren't immediately apparent. Sometimes you may need to dig a little deeper or take a little more time to think. You'll be grateful you did, because you will have tapped into God's revelation-light in greater measure!

Experience is meant to help you do just that: experience God's heart for you personally. It will help you live out God's Word by applying it to your unique life situation. Each question in this section is designed to bring the Bible into your world in fresh, exciting, and relevant ways. At the end of this section, you will have a better idea of how to make choices and decisions that please God, while walking through life on clear paths bathed in the light of his revelation!

The final section is *Share*. God's Word isn't meant to be merely studied or memorized; it's meant to be shared with other people—both through living and telling. This section helps you understand how the reading relates to growing closer to others, to enriching your fellowship and relationship with your world. It also helps you listen to the stories of those around you, so you can bridge Jesus' story with their stories.

SUGGESTIONS FOR INDIVIDUAL STUDY

Reading and studying the Bible is an exciting journey! It's like reading your favorite novel—where the purpose is encountering the heart and mind of the author through its characters and conflict, plot points, and prose.

This study is designed to help you encounter the heart of God and let his Word to you reach deep down into your very soul—all so you can live and enjoy the life he intends for you. And like with any journey, a number of practices will help you along the way:

1. Begin your lesson time in prayer, asking God to open up his Word to you in new ways, show areas of your heart that need teaching and healing, and correct any area in which you're living contrary to his desires for your life.

2. Read the opening section to gain an understanding of the major themes of the reading and ideas for each lesson.

3. Read through the Scripture passage once, underlining or noting in your Bible anything that stands out to you. Reread the passage again, keeping in mind these three questions: What did you notice, perhaps for the first time? What questions do you have? What did you learn about the heart of God?

4. Write your answers to the questions in this Bible study guide or another notebook. If you do get stuck, first ask God to reveal his Word to you and guide you in his truth. And then, either wait until your small group time or ask your pastor or another respected leader for help.

5. Use the end of the lesson to focus your time of prayer, thanking and praising God for the truth of his Word, for what he has revealed to you, and for how he has impacted your daily life.

SUGGESTIONS FOR SMALL GROUP STUDY

The goal of this study is to understand God's Word for you and your community in greater measure, while encountering his heart along the way. A number of practices will also help your group as you journey together:

1. Group studies usually go better when everyone is prepared to participate. The best way to prepare is to come having read the lesson's Scripture reading beforehand. Following the suggestions in each individual study will enrich your time as a community as well.

2. Before you begin the study, your group should nominate a leader to guide the discussion. While this person should work through the questions beforehand, his or her main job isn't to lecture, but to help move the conversation along by asking the lesson questions and facilitating the discussion.

3. This study is meant to be a community affair where everyone shares. Be sure to listen well, contribute where you feel led, and try not to dominate the conversation.

4. The number one rule for community interaction is: nothing is off-limits! No question is too dumb; no answer is out of bounds. While many questions in this study have "right" answers, most are designed to push you and your friends to explore the passage more deeply and understand what it means for daily living.

5. Finally, be ready for God to reveal himself through the passage being discussed and through the discussion that arises out of the group he's put together. Pray that he would reveal his heart and revelation-light to you all in deeper ways. And be open to being challenged, corrected, and changed.

Again, we pray and trust that this Bible study will kindle in you a burning, passionate desire for God and his heart, while impacting your life for years to come. May it open wide the storehouse of heaven's revelation-light. May it reveal new and greater insights into the mysteries of God and the kingdom-realm life he has for you. And may you encounter the heart of God in more fresh and relevant ways than you ever thought possible!

Introduction
to the Gospel of Matthew

Journey into the fulfillment of the Jewish story by diving deep into the Jesus story. Matthew is a natural bridge between the Old and the New Testaments because it is the most Jewish in character. From the first verse to the last, Matthew establishes Jesus as a direct descendant of King David and portrays him as the new, greater Moses.

In fulfilling the Jewish story, Jesus not only upheld the Jewish Torah (Law) but intensified it—not in a legalistic way, but in a spiritual way, because following his teachings is the way into his heavenly kingdom-realm. Unlike any other gospel, Matthew revealed how to live as a citizen of God's kingdom with Jesus as our loving King. From his famous sermon on the hillside to his spiritual stories to his arguments with the Jewish leaders to his compassion for the Jewish crowds, God's kingdom-realm is unveiled before us. Ultimately, Christ's death and resurrection paved the way for us to participate in this realm as full sons and daughters of the King!

We've designed this study to help you explore this King and his kingdom through Matthew's detailed, historical biography of history's most fascinating person, Jesus of Nazareth. Jesus said, "Everyone who hears my teaching and applies it to his life can be compared to a wise man who built his house on an unshakable foundation" (Matthew 7:24). Let's explore those teachings now and find out how to build a life that lasts and matters.

Lesson 1

God Became One of Us

MATTHEW 1:1–4:25

"Listen! A virgin will be pregnant,
she will give birth to a Son, and he will be
known as 'Emmanuel,' which means in Hebrew,
God became one of us." (Matthew 1:23)

Matthew's gospel launches his exciting account into the early life and ministry of the Anointed One with a history lesson. He reveals that the birth of Jesus is rooted in two important ancient Jewish ancestors: Abraham and David.

We first meet Abraham in Genesis 12, when God called him as the vessel through whom he would bless the world by birthing a nation—the nation of Israel. Then there's David, the beloved king of Israel to whom the Lord promised in 2 Samuel 7 that his reign would never end. Matthew's genealogy presents the legal claim that Jesus is King through the line of David, all the way back to the promises given to Abraham.

These promises were the same promises given to humanity in Genesis at the beginning of our story: An Anointed Seed would rescue and re-create the world! But this Seed was far different than the one Israel had expected. While they looked for a mighty human to set things right, God took matters into his own hands by becoming one of the humblest humans ever known.

Keep reading to discover and follow the God-became-one-of-us God who is also our loving King!

Discover the Heart of God

- After reading Matthew 1:1–4:25, what did you notice, perhaps for the first time? What questions do you have? What did you learn about the heart of God?

- In the prophecies throughout the Hebrew Scriptures,[1] the Messiah was promised to Israel to save her and renew the world. When this Messiah finally came, who responded appropriately and who didn't?

---

1   The term Hebrew Scriptures refers to the Old Testament. The Old Testament was composed of the Scriptures of the Jews, and the vast majority of it was written in the Hebrew language—hence the designation Hebrew Scriptures.

• In chapter 3, there are four baptisms. What are they? (Refer to the footnote for Matthew 3:15 if you need help.)

• What were the three ways Satan tempted Jesus? What did Jesus say in response? List what Jesus quoted in response to Satan's three temptations.

• When Jesus came across two sets of brothers, what did he say to them? What did he promise?

Explore the Heart of God

- The genealogy given by Matthew presents the legal claim that Jesus is King through the line of David, all the way back to the promises given to Abraham. Why is this significant? What does this genealogy say about Jesus and about the heart of God?

- Read and reflect on the promises God gave Abraham in Genesis 12:1–3; 22:18 and David in 2 Samuel 7:11–16; Psalm 89:3–4. How do they explain what Jesus came to do in fulfillment of these promises?

- In Matthew 3:15–17, we have the biblical picture of the Christian belief called the Trinity.[2] What is this belief and why is it significant?

---

2 The Christian teaching of the Trinity is that the one and only God exists as three Persons in unity— Father, Son, and Holy Spirit, all of whom share the exact same divine nature.

- Jesus was tempted forty days in the wilderness, which mirrors the forty years Israel wandered in the wilderness after the Exodus. Compare how God's national children responded to their wilderness experience to how God's beloved Son responded to his.[3]

- Why do you think it was important that Jesus began his ministry in Galilee, the land of the Gentiles, instead of Jerusalem, the center of the Jewish people? What does this reveal about the heart of God?

- In 4:23, we find a sort of summary of Jesus' ministry. What are the three primary things Jesus did? Why is the third one especially important, and what does it show?

---

3   If you are unfamiliar with the Jews' wilderness wanderings, read Exodus 15:22-20:26; 32:1-40:38; Numbers 10-14. These passages will give you a good sense of how they handled their experience. Hebrews 3:7-11 provides God's summary commentary on how the Jews behaved.

Experience the Heart of God

- How do you think it must have felt to be Miriam[4] and Joseph? Has there ever been anything the Lord has asked you to do that seemed crazy and scary? How did you respond and what happened?

- It is clear from Matthew 2 that God protected Miriam, Joseph, and Jesus. Consider a dangerous or confusing time in your own life. How did you see God manifest himself to protect and guide you?

- John's condemnation of the religious leaders of his day in 3:7–9 seems harsh. Why do you think he said these things? Could his words apply to the religious systems and leaders of our day?

---

4   "Miriam" is a literal rendering from the original Greek and Aramaic, which leave the Hebrew as is. Miriam is more widely known as Mary, the mother of Jesus.

- In response to each temptation, Jesus quoted Scripture. What might this response say about the importance of God's Word in your own life? How prepared are you to respond to Satan's temptations the way Jesus responded to his?

- Consider your own response to the "Come follow me" call Jesus has given to you. How have you responded? What do you see in Jesus? What are you hoping to find?

Share the Heart of God

- Matthew's genealogy of Jesus in chapter 1 shows that from the very beginning God has been on a mission to rescue and re-create the world. What does this tell us about the heart of God for people you know?

- Part of John's purpose was to prepare the way for the coming Messiah, Jesus, so others could accept and receive him. How might it look in your own life to follow in John's footsteps, by preparing the way for people around you to receive Christ?

- At the beginning of his ministry, Jesus called several men to come and follow him, promising to transform them "into men who catch people for God" (4:19). Take time to pray that he would make the same transformation in your own life!

CONSIDER THIS

Jesus is Emmanuel, showing us that God is with us. He is who every person has been waiting for their whole lives, whether he or she knows it or not. Thank God for sending his Son to be the one who meets our deepest needs. And recommit your own life to answering Jesus' call to "Come follow me."

Lesson 2

Jesus' Sermon on the Good Life

MATTHEW 5:1–7:29

"Everyone who hears my teaching and applies it to his life
can be compared to a wise man who built his house on
an unshakable foundation." (Matthew 7:24)

What is the so-called "good life"? Is it the right combination of career, job, and relationships? Is it about numbers—degrees, cars, money? Does what we say or do matter most? Is it all of the above? Jesus cuts through the confusion and misinformation with probably the most famous sermon ever: his Sermon on the Hillside.

After enduring temptations and calling people to follow him, Jesus launched his ministry by explaining the kind of life for which we all long for—heaven's kingdom-realm. This realm is the good life, where the spiritually impoverished, the peacemakers, and the persecuted are blessed; those who love their enemies are the ones God esteems; and where there's no cause for worry. Its essence lies in loving people as we'd want to be loved; the way to it is narrow, difficult, and few find it.

While everyone is searching for something, what they need is the *good life* Jesus speaks of, the kind of life that's wise and that lasts. So take a seat next to Jesus and give him your ear, for the sermon he's about to preach will change your life for all eternity!

Discover the Heart of God

- After reading Matthew 5:1–7:29, what did you notice, perhaps for the first time? What questions do you have? What did you learn about the heart of God?

- What are the eight themes of blessing Jesus gave in 5:3–10?

- In 5:21–48 Jesus said, "You were taught" but "I say to you" with regards to six different acts. What are they, and what does Jesus teach that strengthens the original instructions?

• In the Lord's Prayer in 6:9–13, Jesus showed us how to love God and others by praying for six things. List those areas Jesus invites us to pray for.

• How did Jesus say you can spot phony prophets?

• On the day of judgment, Jesus said he'll say to some people that he never knew them, though they claimed to do things in his name. Why did he say this will be the case?

Explore the Heart of God

- The Aramaic word for "blessing" is *toowayhon*[1], which means "enriched, great happiness, fortunate, delighted, blissful, contented, blessed, abundant goodness." How does this knowledge enhance the meaning of 5:3–11? What was Jesus saying about the path to life's deepest, abundant goodness?

- In what way did Jesus "fulfill and bring to perfection all that has been written about" (5:17) in the Law of Moses? Why does it matter that he has?

---

1   The Bible as we know it was originally written in Hebrew, Aramaic, and Greek. In recent years, there have been many new discoveries regarding these original manuscripts, especially the Aramaic ones of the New Testament in addition to the Greek. The Aramaic texts are an important added "lens" through which to view God's original Word to us.

- In 5:29–30, Jesus said that if our eye causes us to sin to cut it out, if our hand causes us to sin to cut it off. Doesn't this sound extreme? What do you think Jesus meant here, and why did he call us to this kind of radical living?

- Interestingly, one of Jesus' most frequent commands in the gospels is "Do not worry!" Why do you suppose that is? Why did he say we don't have to worry?

- People often quote 7:1 to say that we should never judge. If you read 7:1–5 closely, you'll see Jesus said something else. What was he saying about judging, evaluating our own flaws, and dealing with other people's "blind spots"?

- Jesus said reality is like two things: a narrow gate and broad path. One leads to eternal life, the other to destruction. Create a list of "narrow gate" and "broad path" ways of living. Based on this list, why do you think so few people find eternal life?

Experience the Heart of God

- Which of Jesus' "blessings" do you most identify with right now? Which apply to your life most?

- Which of Jesus' five teachings in 5:21–48 are most challenging for you? Why?

- Jesus declared, "You can't worship the true God and the god of money!" (6:24). How might money and earthly treasures distract us from true worship?

- What causes you the most worry? How might it look in your life to instead chase after the realm of God's kingdom and trust your heavenly Father to provide for you?

- At the end of his sermon, Jesus described two kinds of houses, which symbolize two kinds of lives. Which "house" are you build-ing? Is it wisely founded on solid rock or foolishly built on sinking sand? Explain.

- Which of Jesus' teachings from this sermon "daze" and "over-whelm" you, as they did the crowds?

Share the Heart of God

- How might sharing the "blessings" in 5:3–12 be an encouragement to people in your life?

- Jesus calls his followers to be "salt" and "light" in their world. In what ways can you live out this calling in your own world in order to share the heart of God?

- How hard is it for you to forgive others? Is there anyone with whom you need to share the heart of God by offering forgiveness?

- Jesus' sermon on the hillside is a tough sermon. Yet it sheds God's revelation-light on what the good life truly is. How might sharing this sermon with people advance the cause of sharing the heart of God?

CONSIDER THIS

Jesus said that everyone who hears his teachings and applies them to their life is wise. But everyone who hears them and doesn't apply them is foolish. Consider the kind of life you are building. Ask the Holy Spirit to search and reveal your heart. Invite him to lead you into heaven's kingdom-realm.

Lesson 3

———

Like Sheep without a Shepherd

MATTHEW 8:1–9:38

When he saw the vast crowds of people,
Jesus' heart was deeply moved with compassion,
because they seemed weary and helpless,
like wandering sheep without a shepherd. (Matthew 9:36)

Sheep are interesting animals. They'll eat anything they can get their jaws onto. They are a species easily preyed upon, so they panic easily and are quick to flee. They have little individuality, preferring to "flock." And some studies even put their IQ just below pigs and on par with cattle. It's no wonder Jesus frequently referred to people as sheep!

His description wasn't meant to be mocking or snide. Instead, he said it out of compassion. For when Jesus saw people, his heart was deeply moved with compassion, then he acted on that compassion. From a leper who was desperate for healing to a Roman official's son who was suffering terribly, from an entire town in need of healing to a boat full of disciples who needed help, from demon-possessed people to blind and mute men—Jesus' heart was deeply moved with compassion for them all because they were weary, burdened, helpless, wandering sheep-like people.

If you think about it, we're no different! This lesson will reveal to you the loving, gentle, caring, and compassionate Shepherd who is ready to demonstrate God's power for you and your life.

Discover the Heart of God

- After reading Matthew 8:1–9:38, what did you notice, perhaps for the first time? What questions do you have? What did you learn about the heart of God?

- According to 9:2, what was it that triggered Jesus' forgiveness and healing of the paraplegic man?

- At the end of Matthew 9, why was Jesus' heart moved deeply with compassion?

- How did the demons respond when Jesus confronted them?

- Why did the townsfolk urge Jesus to go away and leave them alone?

- What did Jesus say healed both the two blind men and the woman who touched his prayer shawl?

Explore the Heart of God

- Both the leper and Roman officer were considered unclean by the religious leaders and customs of Jesus' day. What does it say about Jesus that he defied those religious customs by being with and touching them? What does it say about his intentions and heart toward all people?

- Matthew 8:14–16 said Jesus spent his time healing lots of people: "everyone who was sick received their healing!" What does this show us about Jesus' compassion and God's heart?

- Why do you think it was significant that Jesus claimed to have authority to forgive sins? Why do you think the religious scholars said that was blasphemy?

- What did Jesus mean in 9:12–13? What does this say about us? How do you think the religious scholars viewed themselves?

- Matthew 8 and 9 give us ten miracles that Jesus performed as signs to prove that he was the Messiah. List them, and then explain how these miracles demonstrate Jesus' authority and power over specific things in this world.

Experience the Heart of God

- One of Jesus' would-be followers said he needed to first take care of his father before following Jesus fully. Jesus responded, "Now is the time to follow me" (8:22). What are the things we often say that get in the way of following Jesus now? How about the things in your life? How might Jesus respond to you?

- Compare the response of the disciples to Jesus' miracle in the violent storm to the response of the leper and Roman officer to his intervention. They all had problems, yet the disciples seemed to respond differently than the other two. What's the difference, and how do you typically respond, when life goes wrong—as the disciples or as the leper and Roman officer?

- Of the many miracles in Matthew 8 and 9, which do you identify with most? With whom do you identify personally? Why?

Share the Heart of God

- It is clear from Matthew 8 and 9 that Jesus longs to restore people physically and spiritually. Amazingly, Jesus calls his followers into the same mission![1] What would it look like for you to follow Jesus in bringing his restoration to the world around you, in both a spiritual and physical sense?

---

1 For example, see 10:5–8 and 28:18–20.

- If Jesus ate with the outcasts of society, who might Jesus dine with today? How might it look in your life to follow Jesus by interacting and spending time with society's outcasts?

- Jesus said the harvest for sharing the heart of God and the message of his kingdom-realm is "huge and ripe." Yet he also said, "There are not enough harvesters to bring it all in" (9:37). Who in your life is "ripe"? How might you volunteer as a "reaper" for Owner of the Harvest, to make an impact in that person's life and others' lives?

CONSIDER THIS

At every turn in this lesson, Jesus healed, released, and restored. The compassionate response we find from Jesus to the many weary, burdened, helpless, wandering sheep-like people is almost unbelievable! Yet this is who Jesus is: our loving, compassionate Shepherd King! Spend time thanking him for the abundant compassion he has shown *you*.

Lesson 4

———

Everyone, Come to Me!

MATTHEW 10:1–12:50

"Are you weary, carrying a heavy burden?
Then come to me. I will refresh your life, for I am your oasis.
Simply join your life with mine. Learn my ways and you'll
discover that I'm gentle, humble, easy to please.
You will find refreshment and rest in me." (Matthew 11:28–29)

From health problems to job problems, marriage problems to financial problems—sometimes life's burdens feel like trying to move an immense boulder up a hill, only to watch it roll back down again.

In today's lesson, you'll learn an amazing truth about Jesus and his life: rather than adding to your burdens, Jesus takes them away! He promises to be an "oasis" for us; that he is "gentle, humble, easy to please"; that we will find the kind of "refreshment and rest" we're all longing for. At every turn in his ministry, Jesus was removing the boulders of blindness and lameness, leprosy and deafness—even the burden of death itself! And remarkably, Jesus called his followers to bring, bear, and *be* this message of refreshment to the world around them.

The life Jesus offers each and every person is a burden-free life. It's a life that's open to everyone. It's also a life we're called to invite others into. Have you joined your life to his? Are you offering that life to others?

Discover the Heart of God

- After reading Matthew 10:1–12:50, what did you notice, perhaps for the first time? What questions do you have? What did you learn about the heart of God?

- What authority did Jesus impart to his disciples? What message did he give them to share?

- Why did Jesus openly denounce certain cities? What did they do wrong?

• How did Jesus say you could recognize whether someone is virtuous or evil?

• Who did Jesus say are his true family members (12:48)?

Explore the Heart of God

• How does 10:1 compare to Matthew 8 and 9? What does this tell you about our mission as Jesus' disciples?

• What did Jesus mean when he said that his coming "will bring conflict and division" (10:34)? How does he bring such conflict?

- What do you think it means to share Jesus' cross and experience it as your own? Can you think of modern examples?

- Why do you think God wants "compassion more than a sacrifice" (12:7) when it comes to our spirituality and faith? What's the difference between compassion and sacrifice?

- Why do you think the Pharisees were so angry Jesus healed on the Sabbath? What does this say about them? What does it say about Jesus?

- What are some examples of virtuous and evil fruit? Make a list to compare the two.

Experience the Heart of God

- Persecution can come in many forms—physical, social, or financial, to name just a few. Have you ever been persecuted for your faith? If so, how? And how can 10:17–18 bring comfort?

- Have you ever had a division in an earthly relationship because of your relationship with Jesus? What was that like? How did it turn out?

- Are you "weary, carrying a heavy burden" (11:28)? How would it look in your life to come to Jesus to find what you need for your life? What would you like him to take from you? What do you need him to give you?

- How does it make you feel to know that you are part of Jesus' true family if you are one of his followers?

Share the Heart of God

- At the beginning of our lesson, Jesus sent out his disciples to do and teach what he was doing and teaching. He still does! How might this look to follow the disciples' lead into ripened harvest fields?

- Why does Jesus say we don't have to be "afraid or intimidated by others" (10:26) when we share the heart of God and story of Jesus?

- Why is 11:29–30 such good news to those you know? Who do you know who is "weary, carrying heavy burdens" (11:28)? Who do you know who needs Jesus to refresh his or her life?

- In 12:1–12, Jesus explains that God cares much more about our compassion and love toward others than our fulfilling religious rituals and duties. How should this impact the way we share the heart of God?

CONSIDER THIS

"Are you weary, carrying a heavy burden?" Jesus asks. If the answer is yes, then come to him! Come find refreshment and rest in your Savior. Bring your boulder-sized burdens to Jesus, asking him to make them lighter and refresh your life. Then consider the ways you can follow the apostles in broadcasting the message of heaven's kingdom-realm, a realm that it is accessible to all and close enough to touch today!

Lesson 5

Jesus' Spiritual Stories

MATTHEW 13:1–53

*He taught them many things by using stories, parables
that would illustrate spiritual truths. (Matthew 13:3)*

It's been shown that storytelling bypasses certain circuits in the brain to put us at ease, create stronger engagement and emotional connections, and open us up to new ideas. Which is why the best teachers are those who use stories to teach a deeper truth. Perhaps this is why Jesus' teaching method of choice to illustrate spiritual truths was stories.

Jesus was the greatest storyteller, because he used short, memorable spiritual stories called *parables*. He used them to communicate deeper truths about the good life we've been exploring in heaven's kingdom-realm. This lesson is filled with them. Jesus taught a story about a farmer who sowed seed on four different soils. Then he shared stories about two of the tiniest elements: mustard seeds and yeast. His stories about hidden treasure and an extraordinary pearl draw our attention to the value of God's kingdom-realm.

Jesus' teachings are so memorable and compelling because he taught using simple, easy-to-follow stories. He weaved together elements from everyday life to teach us about life in heaven's kingdom-realm. Continue our study with a listening, open heart. When you do, Jesus promises you will receive more than enough revelation about what it means to live the good life.

Discover the Heart of God

- After reading Matthew 13:1–53, what did you notice, perhaps for the first time? What questions do you have? What did you learn about the heart of God?

- Why did Jesus say he spoke to people in parables? What did he expect from those who heard the parables, and what did he say they'd receive in response?

- Jesus told a story about four soils. What were the soils, and what did he say they represented?

- Why did Jesus say the harvesters in his parable weren't supposed to uproot the weeds? How did Jesus explain this spiritual story?

- How is heaven's kingdom-realm like a fisherman?

Explore the Heart of God

- What is a parable? Why do you think Jesus taught this way?

- What do you think is the significance of Jesus' parable of the four soils? How should it impact how we live?

• In the Bible, harvesting is often a picture of judgment. Given that context, what do you think the spiritual story in 13:24–30 represents?

• In what ways is heaven's kingdom-realm like a mustard seed and yeast, as in 13:31–33?

• In Jesus' day, the three measures of flour in his parable of the yeast was nearly twenty-two kilos—enough to feed three hundred people! Yet yeast begins so tiny. How is the explosive power and impact of God's kingdom-realm tiny, yet powerful?

- Why is heaven's kingdom-realm like a hidden treasure in a field and a jewel merchant? What do these stories in 13:44–46 illustrate?

Experience the Heart of God

- The story about the four soils represented four different kinds of people. At this moment in your spiritual journey, which soil do you think you are? How do you feel about this?

- Jesus said that when we listen to him with an open heart, we will progressively receive more revelation knowledge until we have more than enough. How do you think it would look in your life to "listen with an open heart" (13:12) in order to experience more of the heart of God?

- How have you personally experienced or witnessed the explosive, transforming growth of God's kingdom-realm?

- Jesus described God's kingdom-realm as being like a hidden treasure or an extraordinary pearl, where people would do anything to get their hands on it. How would it look in your life to do whatever it takes to lay hands on and experience God's kingdom-realm in its fullness?

Share the Heart of God

- Jesus' parable about the four soils has a lot to teach us, not only about how we're living, but about where we're sharing his story. How does this spiritual story relate to our sharing Christ with our world?

- How should Jesus' explanation of the story about the weeds and wheat both encourage us and provoke us to share Christ with our world?

- The principle of the parables of the tiny mustard seed and yeast is that the small and seemingly insignificant things in God's kingdom realm are important; they still have the power to bring change and transformation. How should this encourage you as an agent of God's kingdom-realm, on mission to share his heart?

CONSIDER THIS

Jesus was the greatest storyteller ever because he taught deep truths using everyday things we can all relate to. He said the kingdom's message is like seed that falls on the soil of our hearts. Heaven's kingdom-realm is also like yeast: tiny, yet explosive in its transforming power. It's also infinitely valuable and precious like a rare pearl. Now, all that's left is to respond. How will you?

Lesson 6

———

Jesus-Centered, Cross-Shaped Discipleship

MATTHEW 13:54–16:28

"If you truly want to follow me, you should at once completely reject and disown your own life. And you must be willing to share my cross and experience it as your own, as you continually surrender to my ways." (Matthew 16:24)

When it comes to following Jesus, sometimes it can be downright confusing what exactly that means! Does it require us to recite a certain prayer? What about performing a certain set of religious rituals and duties? Is it about living a certain way, or *not* living another way?

In today's lesson, Jesus paints a very different picture. It has nothing to do with man-made religious activities or a list of *dos* and *don'ts*. Instead, Jesus reveals that our Christian discipleship is entirely Jesus centered and cross shaped. Through a series of episodes, we see that Jesus longs for us to step out by following him in faith. He also has no room for man-made religious traditions and any way we might try and put him in a box to fit our own religious agenda.

In the end, this lesson teaches us a truly remarkable, even startling revelation-truth about what it means to be a disciple of Christ: following Jesus means setting aside our self and our own agenda, walking the way of suffering and sacrifice, and dying to find true life.

Discover the Heart of God

- After reading Matthew 13:54–16:28, what did you notice, perhaps for the first time? What questions do you have? What did you learn about the heart of God?

- How did the people of Gennesaret respond to Jesus when he landed on their shore? Compare their response to the religious leaders of Jesus' day.

- In what way did Jesus say Isaiah 29 described the religious leaders and their religious attitudes? Why did he tell his disciples to avoid them?

- Upon what did Jesus promise to build his church? What did he promise us would happen?

- How did Peter react to the news that Jesus would be executed and raised back from the dead in three days? How did Jesus respond to Peter's reaction? Why?

- Jesus asked, "What are the people saying about me, the Son of Man? Who do they believe I am?" (16:13). What were people saying about him? What did the disciples say about him?

Explore the Heart of God

- Why might it be significant that Jesus wasn't even accepted in his hometown?

- After hearing reports about Jesus, Herod thought he was John come back from the dead! Matthew has already shown similarities between John and Jesus, for example in 3:2 and 4:17. How does the story told in 14:1–12 continue this comparison? What does John's story anticipate about Jesus'?

- In Matthew, we often find Jesus "deeply moved with compassion" toward the crowds or people (e.g., 20:34). Why do you suppose this was? How similar or different is his reaction from your picture of God? Or your picture of the church?

- Peter is often criticized for not having enough faith, yet he was the one who got out of the boat while the other disciples stayed inside! What does Peter's initial response and question to Jesus say about his spiritual journey (14:28-29)? What does what happened after this say about his journey (vv. 30-33)?

- What does Jesus mean in 15:11, that "what truly contaminates a person is not what he puts into his mouth, but what comes out of his mouth"? How is this connected with the religious leaders' accusation of the disciples in 15:1–2?

- In light of 14:13–21, why doesn't the question in 15:33 make sense? What does it show about the disciples' faith?

Experience the Heart of God

- Would you say you are more concerned with what you put into your mouth than what comes out of our mouth? Are you more concerned with performing religious duties with your hands than honoring God with your heart? What's the difference?

- When Jesus provides, he goes all out—giving us enough so that we are "full and satisfied" (15:37). What is it you need Jesus to provide for you? Now, ask him!

- Jesus said the power of death won't be able to overpower the church. In what ways does this promise encourage you in your life as a member of the church?

• How might it look for modern people to share Jesus' cross and experience it as their own? What kinds of things might they have to sacrifice? What about you?

• Jesus asked, "Who do the people say I am?" Who do you say Jesus is?

Share the Heart of God

• Matthew wrote in chapter 13 that even Jesus wasn't honored in his hometown. How might this encourage us when we follow him by sharing the heart of God?

• Jesus had a lot to say about religious hypocrisy. How have you witnessed religious hypocrisy—whether in your life or in others' lives? How does religious hypocrisy impact our ability to share the heart of God?

- Jesus often criticized the Jewish religious leaders for demanding supernatural signs. What kind of signs do people look for nowadays? How could this be harmful to their spiritual journeys?

- In 16:24–25, Jesus outlined a pretty intense description of how it really looks to follow him. Why is it important to be honest about what it truly means to follow Jesus when we share the heart of God?

CONSIDER THIS

Jesus reminds us that the way of self-sacrifice is the only way to find life. It's also the only way we can truly follow him. Close by considering in what ways you might be following him through religious rituals or by holding on to your own agenda. Then ask him to help you share his cross and experience it as your own.

Lesson 7

The King Fully Unveiled

MATTHEW 17:1–18:35

Then Jesus' appearance was dramatically altered....
He was transfigured before their very eyes....
"This is my dearly loved Son, the constant focus of my delight.
Listen to him!" (Matthew 17:2, 5)

Who was Jesus? Was he like one of the ancient sages, dispensing words of wisdom and life-changing teachings? Was he a revolutionary who revolted against the systems and powers of his day, calling us to do the same in our day? Was he a model of how to live and love?

The disciples were wondering the same things! While they had seen Jesus perform amazing miracles and give abundant mercy, their picture of him wasn't yet fully clear. In this lesson, however, three of Jesus' followers got a front-row answer to their questions when he invited them to join him on a mountain. While removed from the rest of the watching world, Jesus was fully unveiled in all his glory before their eyes as the radiant Son of God!

But afterwards, the picture of Jesus' character and what he came to do became even clearer when he spoke about forgiveness in one of his spiritual stories. Forgiveness is perhaps the central virtue of heaven's kingdom-realm, because it is at the very heart of God himself. And Jesus came to offer this forgiveness by offering us himself. Receive the full picture of our Loving King in today's lesson.

Discover the Heart of God

- After reading Matthew 17:1–18:35, what did you notice, perhaps for the first time? What questions do you have? What did you learn about the heart of God?

- What did the voice of God say to Peter the Rock, Jacob[1], and John on a mountain when Jesus was transfigured?

- How did Jesus respond to the disciples' question, "Who is considered to be the greatest in heaven's kingdom-realm?" (18:1)

---

1 "Jacob" is a literal rendering from the original Greek. This disciple is more widely known as James.

- What are the steps Jesus outlines in Matthew 18 when confronting sin in other people?

- How many times did Jesus say Peter should forgive someone? How did Jesus say his heavenly Father would deal with people who didn't offer forgiveness?

Explore the Heart of God

- To whom do you think Jesus was referring when he talked about Elijah in 17:11–12? What was Jesus saying in this passage about his own ministry and the future?

- Why do you think Jesus continued to say how "wayward and wrong this generation is" (17:17)? Who was he referring to, and how did the episode in 17:14–21 illustrate what Jesus kept saying?

- What do you think is Jesus' point when comparing faith to a mustard seed? How should this impact your own life with Christ right now?

- Why did Jesus say we need to be like a "gentle child" to enter the kingdom? What was his point?

• Why does Jesus tell us in 18:17 to disregard unrepentant believers, even so far as to treat them like an "outsider"? Is this too severe, or does it make sense? Explain.

• How did Jesus' spiritual story about the king with servants who borrowed money relate to Peter the Rock's question about forgiveness?

Experience the Heart of God

• One day, three of Jesus' disciples had a remarkable supernatural experience of Jesus, where he was fully unveiled before their eyes. Have you ever had an experience with Jesus where he opened your eyes to a greater revelation of who he is?

- Jesus claimed that a lack of faith hindered the disciples' ability to heal. What might God want to do *for* you and *through* you that a lack of faith might be hindering?

- What drastic measures might Jesus be asking you to take to get rid of sin in your life?

- Describe a time when you were sinned against and needed to forgive someone. What was that like? If you made the choice to forgive, how did you experience the heart of God in greater measure?

Share the Heart of God

- Why is it important to have faith when it comes to sharing the heart of God, like it was in 17:14–20?

- How does it make you feel to know God doesn't want a single believer to be lost?

- Who in your life is difficult to forgive or has been difficult to forgive? How might it look to follow Jesus by sharing the heart of God by forgiving them "seventy times seven times"?

CONSIDER THIS

Jesus said the well of our forgiveness must be unending, and the amount of forgiveness we extend to others will be used to measure God's own forgiveness toward us. Ask the Holy Spirit to reveal your willingness or unwillingness to extend forgiveness. Then pray for his help in forgiving others "seventy times seven times." After all, that's who God is: We forgive because God first forgave us in Christ!

Lesson 8

The Way to Eternal Life

MATTHEW 19:1–20:34

"Wonderful teacher—is there a good work
I have to do to obtain eternal life?" (Matthew 19:16)

What does it take to receive eternal life? This is a good question—perhaps *the* question! Do we have to *say* the right thing, perhaps pray the right prayer? Is *doing* the right thing necessary, perhaps performing the right works, or some amount or combination of works? Does God want us to *act* the right way, to live and act according to a certain set of rules?

One day, a young man asked Jesus this very question. He, too, wondered what he had to do to receive eternal life. But, he wasn't happy with the answer Jesus ultimately gave! In fact, all throughout this lesson, there are ways that Jesus answers this question that seem puzzling and counterintuitive. No one will enter heaven's kingdom-realm unless they become like a child, Jesus said. Then he insisted that the first will be last and the last will be first in his kingdom-realm. He even went so far as to say that in order for us to obtain eternal life, we need to drink his cup of suffering and death!

Ultimately, what we discover in this lesson is that God wants our *heart*—all of it! That's what it takes to receive eternal life.

Discover the Heart of God

- After reading Matthew 19:1–20:34, what did you notice, perhaps for the first time? What questions do you have? What did you learn about the heart of God?

- What sin does Jesus say people commit who divorce for any reason other than sexual immorality? Why do you think this is the case?

- What was it that Jesus said the rich man lacked when it came to obeying the law fully to obtain eternal life?

- Why do you think Jesus reassured Peter of his reward when Peter claimed to have given up everything to follow him?

- In Jesus' spiritual story about the landowner and laborers, what did the landowner pay each of the laborers who started working at daybreak, nine, three, and five o'clock?

Explore the Heart of God

- What were the three types of celibates Jesus mentioned in 19:12? How do you think this relates to his teachings on marriage and sexual purity?

- In Jesus' day, children were at the bottom of the social ladder and not highly regarded. How does this background information inform how the disciples and Jesus responded to the children at hand?

- What do you think were the rich man's true intentions when he asked Jesus his question about eternal life? How do people reflect those intentions in our own day?

- What do you think is the meaning of Jesus' parable about the landowner and laborers? Who do the landowner and laborers represent? How do you feel about the landowner paying everyone an equal amount, even to those who worked fewer hours?

- Jacob and John naively declared they were able to endure "the baptism into death." Their ambition was emphasized by having their mother come to ask that they be placed in a high position. This event followed immediately after Jesus prophesied for the third time about his coming crucifixion. In what way was their ambitious request significant, especially in relation to 20:17–19?

- How did the Son of Man "not come expecting to be served by everyone, but to serve everyone" (20:28)?

Experience the Heart of God

- Have you ever been personally affected by divorce or the results of divorce? What was that like? What do you think might happen in our society—even in the church—if we took Jesus' marriage ethics more seriously?

- Why do you think it's difficult for people who "have it all" to enter into heaven's kingdom-realm? What might you need to give up to fully enter yourself?

- What do you think about the request Jacob and John's mother made to Jesus? What do you think about Jesus' response?

- "What do you want me to do for you?" is a question Jesus continues to ask us all. How would you answer it for yourself?

Share the Heart of God

- Jesus' teachings on divorce seem pretty countercultural. But how might sharing God's heart for marriage as revealed in 19:1–12 be helpful to people you know?

- We all know people who are far from God and seem like hopeless cases. Yet Jesus said otherwise! Why should 19:26 encourage us to continue sharing the heart of God with them?

- How do you feel about the idea that God will give the same gift of eternal life to all people equally at the end of the age, regardless of how long they've been following Jesus? How might this influence what you share with others about God's grace and love to them?

- God longs to do for others what he did for the two blind men in 20:30–34. Who do you know who needs God to do something for them? Spend time praying for their healing, release, and restoration.

CONSIDER THIS

How are you seeking eternal life and the heart of God? Like a little child, in humility and service? Or in pride and self-justification, like the wealthy young man? As you end this lesson, pledge to do what the young man couldn't do: Give yourself to Jesus fully and follow him for the rest of your life!

Lesson 9

The Beginning of Jesus' End

MATTHEW 21:1–22:46

"Bring the victory, Lord, Son of David!
He comes with the blessings of being sent
from the Lord Yahweh! We celebrate with praises
to God in the highest!" (Matthew 21:9)

It's been said there are only three ways to view Jesus: as a liar, a lunatic, or Lord. How did people view him during his day? It's clear throughout Matthew, but especially from this lesson, that it was a mixed bag!

The religious leaders definitely thought he was a liar—not only because he claimed to be the Messiah, but especially because he claimed to be equal with Yahweh! They challenged his authority and tried to entrap him in his own teachings. They also thought he was a lunatic—what else would they have thought after he drove away the merchants from the temple and overturned their tables? Or when he received the praise of children shouting that he was the Son of David?

Still others thought he was Lord. His disciples sure did, but so did the crowds. "Bring the victory, Lord, Son of David!" they shouted when he arrived in Jerusalem on the way to the cross. "He comes with the blessings of being sent from the Lord Yahweh!"

How do you view Jesus? Here's a more important question: How are you responding to him? Keep reading to discover more revelation-light about our Loving King.

Discover the Heart of God

- After reading Matthew 21:1–22:46, what did you notice, perhaps for the first time? What questions do you have? What did you learn about the heart of God?

- When Jesus arrived in Jerusalem, what animal did he ride in on? What was the response and reaction of the crowd to his arrival? What was the response of the religious leaders to the children's cry, "Blessings and praise to the Son of David!" (21:15-16)?

- When Jesus entered Jerusalem, where did he go and what did he do?

- Describe the parable Jesus told about the two sons, and what happened. What happened in the next parable, the one about the rejected son?

- What did Jesus say is the greatest commandment?

Explore the Heart of God

- Why was the animal Jesus rode into Jerusalem significant? What does this say about Jesus and his mission?

- Compare what was happening in the temple courts before Jesus' act and what happened afterwards. Why was this before-and-after picture so significant to Jesus' mission as well as the heart of God?

- In the Old Testament, a fig tree often symbolized Israel. Knowing this, what might be the significance of what Jesus was saying and doing in 21:18–22?

- Who do the two sons represent in Jesus' spiritual story in 21:28–32?

- Describe what happened in the parable of the wedding feast. What excuse did the invited guests give for not attending? Who do you think the king, the invited guests, the son, and the people of the streets represent? What do you think was meant by the parable's ending, and what reality does it point to and represent?

• How did Jesus respond to the Pharisees' question regarding whether it was proper for Jews to pay taxes to Caesar? Why do you think his response was so significant for his day, knowing that Israel lived under imperial Roman occupation?

Experience the Heart of God

• What excuses do people often give for not receiving Jesus and becoming his follower? Are you giving any excuses?

• What does Jesus' teaching on taxes say about our Christian responsibility to our own government?

- Do you ever feel like the religious leaders and crowds—dazed and stunned by Jesus' words? What has he said so far that has seemed stunning to you?

- How do you think it looks to faithfully live and obey Jesus' "greatest commandment"? How would it look for you to obey it in your own life?

Share the Heart of God

- When Jesus arrived in Jerusalem, in order to fully share the heart of God, he kicked out the merchants and money changers who had set up barriers in the temple. What similar religious barriers might we need to "overturn" in order to share God's heart more fully?

• What does it tell us about the heart of God that "many sinners, tax collectors, and prostitutes are going into God's kingdom-realm ahead of" the religious elite (21:31)? Why is this good news for those we know?

• What does the wedding feast story in 22:1–14 mean for those we share God's heart with who might want to show up at Christ' banquet on their own terms?

• Jesus said that one aspect of the "greatest commandment" is to "love your friend in the same way you love yourself" (22:39). In what practical ways can you live this out as you share the heart of God?

CONSIDER THIS

We can reject Jesus as a liar or lunatic, or we can receive him as Lord. He leaves us no other choice. Pay close attention to this lesson, especially Jesus' spiritual stories. Because, as Psalm 118 says, "The very stone the builder rejected as flawed has now become the most important capstone of the arch."

Lesson 10

Live Always Ready for the End

MATTHEW 23:1–25:46

"So always be ready, alert, and prepared,
because at an hour when you're not expecting him,
the Son of Man will come." (Matthew 24:44)

Every great story eventually comes to an end. The story of humankind is no different. For millennia, generations have been predicting and wondering about the end of the world as we know it. Including Christians.

While Jesus said we shouldn't speculate about exact times and dates because only the Father knows them, he did offer some clarity. He offered signs that point to the end, including earthquakes, diseases, and famine. He said there would be widespread persecution of believers. He taught several spiritual stories to help us prepare. Ultimately though, Jesus' emphasis wasn't about the end, but about the present: He told us to live *now* in light of the end, warning what might happen to us if we don't. Always be "ready, alert, and prepared" right now, Jesus insisted, because you never know when he will return.

Let Christ's teachings in this lesson impress themselves upon you, so that you can live rightly in these last days. Live in anticipation of the end of this chapter and the beginning of the next in God's grand story!

Discover the Heart of God

- After reading Matthew 23:1–25:46, what did you notice, perhaps for the first time? What questions do you have? What did you learn about the heart of God?

- Jesus said "great sorrow" awaited the Jewish religious leaders for seven reasons. What were those reasons?

- What did Jesus say in response to the disciples' question about what supernatural signs they should expect to signal his return?

- How did Jesus say we should respond to reports about the return of the Messiah? How did Jesus describe the return of the Son of Man and what will happen?

- Why was the master angered by what he heard from the servant entrusted with one thousand gold coins? What did he do to him?

Explore the Heart of God

- How do you think Christian teachers and believers can guard themselves against the dangers of not practicing what they preach, like the religious teachers of Jesus' day?

- What seven things do you think Christians can take away from Jesus' teachings about the seven "great sorrows"? Explain, and apply them to our lives today.

- Why do you think it's necessary to "keep your hope to then end" (24:13)? How does this look, practically?

• What response did the master give to the servants entrusted to 5,000 and 2,000 gold coins? Why is it significant that these responses were the same for each person? What might be the deeper spiritual meaning of this spiritual story on financial stewardship?

• In Jesus' parable about the sheep and goats, who do these animals represent? Why does he separate them, and why is it significant?

• Matthew 25:40 has often been misunderstood as referring to poor people. But the "little ones" seem to refer to Jesus' brothers and sisters, his followers. What was he saying about people who refuse to welcome and embrace his people?

Experience the Heart of God

- Which of the "great sorrows" might you need to personally guard against?

- What did Jesus say about our ability to know the day the world will end? How should this impact our daily living and experience of the heart of God?

- How can people keep their hearts burning with spiritual passion? How can they keep their hearts from going cold?

- How would it look in your life to be "ready, alert, and prepared" for the Son of Man's appearance?

Share the Heart of God

- How do you think it looks to put Jesus' teaching from 23:11–12 into practice in order to share the heart of God?

- How does it make you feel to know that Jesus will divide people into two groups at the end of the age? What urgency does this reality pose for you and those you know, especially the urgency to share the heart of God?

CONSIDER THIS

There will come a day when Jesus returns, when the last chapter of our world's story will come to a close and a whole new story will begin. As the church's ancient creed declares, "He will come again in glory to judge the living and the dead." Ask the Holy Spirit to prepare you for that day, to keep watch for Christ's return, and to be ready for him when he does.

Lesson 11

———

Our Crushed Passover Lamb

MATTHEW 26:1–27:10

"My heart is overwhelmed and crushed with grief.
It feels as though I'm dying.... My Father, if there is any way
you can deliver me from this suffering, please take it from me.
Yet what I want is not important, for I only desire to fulfill
your plan for me." (Matthew 26:38–39)

There is a fascinating piece to Jesus' story that is often overlooked: Jesus died during Passover. Do you know the deep meaning behind this ancient Jewish festival? Its origin stretches all the way back to Israel's exodus.

Recall the story of Moses and the Jewish people who were enslaved in Egypt. God called Moses to tell Pharaoh to let his people go, but Pharaoh refused. He continued refusing throughout several plagues until finally, God caused all the firstborn of in the land of Egypt to die—except the Israelites. For God provided a way to save their lives by shedding the blood of an innocent lamb (Exodus 12:3-4). The lamb's blood was smeared over the beams of their home's front door. When God saw the blood, he *passed over* his judgment—they were saved. This act foreshadowed the ultimate blood sacrifice, when hundreds of years later, Jesus would become the Passover Lamb for all humankind.

Today, we see Jesus looking toward his sacrifice. He is anointed for death, and he anticipates it by celebrating the Passover meal, which memorialized that first sacrifice in Egypt. He knew the suffering he would face, yet he only wanted to fulfill God's plan for salvation. Because Jesus' blood was smeared over the beams of the cross, God's judgment *passes over* us—we are saved!

Discover the Heart of God

• After reading Matthew 26:1–27:10, what did you notice, perhaps for the first time? What questions do you have? What did you learn about the heart of God?

• Why were the disciples annoyed with the woman who poured perfume over Jesus' head? How did Jesus respond?

• When Jesus and the disciples ate the Passover meal, Jesus broke bread and passed a cup of wine. To what did Jesus compare these table elements? What did Jesus say they would accomplish?

- What kind of emotions did Jesus experience in the garden of Gethsemane? What did Jesus say to his Father when he prayed?

- Ultimately, what charge did the religious leaders bring against Jesus?

Explore the Heart of God

- Looking back to the Old Testament, what was the significance of the Passover meal? Why was Jesus' death that much more significant since it happened around this important Jewish holiday?

- How many times did Jesus say Peter would deny him? Does this come true? Compare this event to Peter's restoration in John 21.

• How does Jesus' experience in the garden enhance or further define the sweet reality of our salvation, especially in light of 26:39, 42?

• Jesus said he could have asked his Father for an angel army to rescue him, but didn't. Why not? What does this say about his commitment to his mission? To us?

• Compare the two responses of Peter and Judas after their individual betrayals. How are they similar? How are they different?

Experience the Heart of God

- Given the significance of the Lord's Supper as Jesus describes it in 26:26–29, how should you respond every time you eat the bread and drink the cup of the Lord's Table? How has it impacted your life?

- How do you think Jesus must have felt when his friends fell asleep and then Judas gave him that kiss? Have you ever experienced this kind of relational betrayal? What was that like, how did you feel?

- When Jesus was arrested to be crucified, he said that if he wanted to, he could summon twelve angel armies to come to his rescue. Yet he didn't. How should this realization impact your experience of the heart of God?

- Have you ever denied Jesus like Peter did—whether in word or deed? How did it feel afterwards?

Share the Heart of God

- Paul said that every time Christians celebrate the Lord's Supper, they proclaim the death and resurrection of Jesus. How can this meal be the perfect occasion to share the heart of God with the world?

- Before Jesus was crucified, he spent time in a garden, praying to his Father while his heart was "overwhelmed and crushed with grief." (26:38). What does this tell us about God's heart for people in your life, that Jesus still went to the cross?

CONSIDER THIS

Biblically, the original Jewish New Year begins in the month of the Passover festival, as Exodus 12 says. How appropriate that the new era God's people dawned that same month with a new Passover through the blood of Jesus! Contemplate all that you have received because Jesus went to the cross as the final Passover Lamb—for you and for the world.

Lesson 12

Jesus' Death, Our Commissioning

MATTHEW 27:11–28:20

"All the authority of the universe has been
given to me. Now go in my authority and make
disciples of all nations." (Matthew 28:18–19)

In the ancient world, the death of a major hero was considered the climax of their life. In stories about these beloved characters, special focus was paid in retelling the manner and nature of their death, which revealed their true character.

The same was true of Jesus and the way the early church told, retold, and told again of his death. In fact, early Christians shared this part of his story the earliest and most often. Perhaps that's why the Gospels often feel like a Passion narrative with an extended introduction! In Matthew's retelling, we find a detailed account of Jesus' death. From his trial before Pilate to his condemnation to death, from his crucifixion to his last cry on the cross—even the violent earthquake leads to a testimony of Jesus' true character by a Roman military officer: "There is no doubt, this man was the Son of God!" (27:54).

But of course, death didn't have the final word in Jesus' story, for he rose again in full resurrection glory, bearing all authority and power and dominion! Because this is true of Jesus, it's also true of us—the church of

Jesus Christ is sent in the same power to continue the magnificent mission of our loving King.

Discover the Heart of God

- After reading Matthew 27:11–28:20, what did you notice, perhaps for the first time? What questions do you have? What did you learn about the heart of God?

- How did Jesus respond to the charges brought against him?

- Describe what happened to Jesus leading up to the actual crucifixion. What happened when Jesus "gave up his Spirit" (27:50)?

- What happened when the two Miriams[1] went to visit Jesus' body in the tomb?

- The authority of Jesus has sent us on mission to do what three things?

Explore the Heart of God

- What did Jesus say to God the Father while on the cross? What does this say about what Jesus experienced and felt through the course of his crucifixion?

---

1   "Miriam" is a literal rendering from the original Greek and Aramaic, which leave the Hebrew as is. The two "Miriams" referenced here are more widely known as Mary, the mother of James, and Mary Magdalene.

- Why is it significant that the veil in the Holy of Holies split down the middle from top to bottom (see Hebrews 9:3; 10:19-23)? What does it symbolize and literally mean for every Christian?

- After Jesus' burial, what did the religious leaders ask of Pilate? Why is this fact important when it came to what happened just days later?

- When the disciples met Jesus on the mountainside, some worshiped, yet some doubted. How does 28:18–20 confront those doubts?

Experience the Heart of God

- One of the results of Jesus' crucifixion is that there is no more veil separating us from God. Why does this matter, and what does this mean for how you can experience the heart of God and your relationship with him?

- The Christian church believes that on the cross, Jesus Christ died to pay the penalty for our sins—he died in our place. What does the cross mean for you personally? How have you experienced the heart of God when contemplating the cross?

- The Christian church also believes that the resurrection of Jesus was the catalyst for our own new, restored lives today. How have you experienced the heart of God through Christ's resurrection? How do you want to experience Jesus' new life right now?

- How should the reality that Jesus has been given all authority and that he is with us every day encourage our walk with him?

Share the Heart of God

- How is the cross truly good news for the people you know who are far from God? How might it look in your life to share this good news with them so they too can share in the heart of God?

- Why should the resurrection of Jesus take center place when we share the heart of God? What does his resurrection offer to those you know?

- In what way should 28:18–20 be the wind in our sails for sharing the heart of God with our world?

CONSIDER THIS

Unlike all the other ancient heroes, our Hero-God Jesus Christ lives again, and his life continues on in us! After all, it's why we're called the body of Christ: We continue Christ's mission as his eyes and ears, hands and feet. Now go and influence people in such a way that they give their lives and lifestyles to Jesus as their Loving King. And know that Jesus is with you every step of the way!

Encounter the Heart of God

The Passion Translation Bible is a new, heart-level translation that expresses God's fiery heart of love to this generation, using Hebrew, Greek, and Aramaic manuscripts and merging the emotion and life-changing truth of God's Word. If you are hungry for God and want to know him on a deeper level, The Passion Translation will help you encounter God's heart and discover what he has for your life.

The Passion Translation box set
includes the following eight books:

Psalms: Poetry on Fire

Proverbs: Wisdom from Above

Song of Songs: Divine Romance

Matthew: Our Loving King

John: Eternal Love

Luke and Acts: To the Lovers of God

Hebrews and James: Faith Works

**Letters from Heaven: From the
Apostle Paul** (Galatians, Ephesians,
Philippians, Colossians, I & II Timothy)

Additional titles available include:

Mark: Miracles and Mercy
Romans: Grace and Glory
1 & 2 Corinthians: Love and Truth

THE
PASSION
TRANSLATION

thePassionTranslation.com